SCHOOL MEMORIES JOURNAL

Pre-K To 12th Grade

Attach Pictures Of Fun Moments

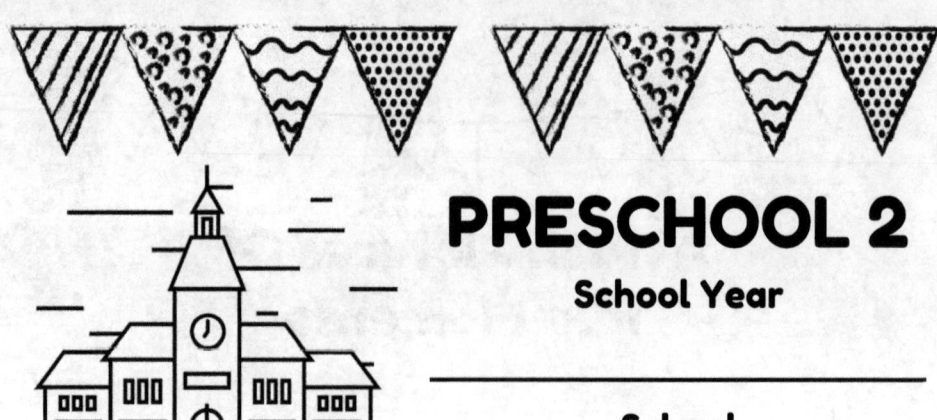

PRESCHOOL 2

School Year

_____

School

_____

Attach Your Photo

This School Year, I Am Looking Forward To...

_____

_____

_____

My Teacher's Name is

_____

The Things I Bring To School Are...

_____

_____

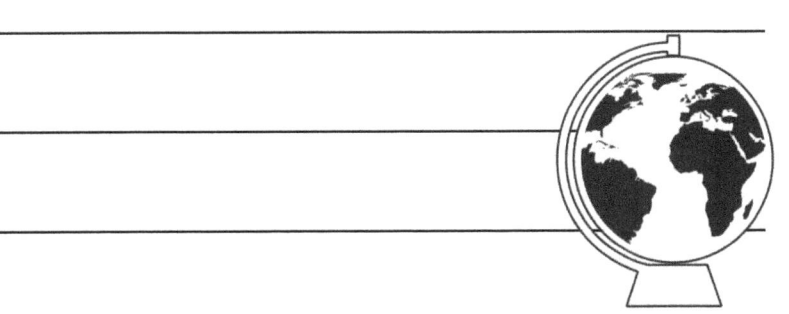

When I Arrive At School, The First Thing I Do Is...

_____

_____

During Recess, I...

_____

_____

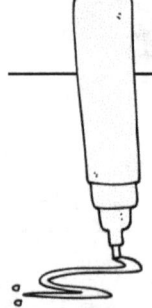
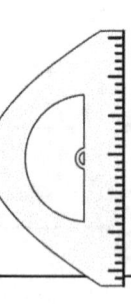

My Favorite Games To Play Are

_____

_____

_____

My New Friends This Year Are...

_____

_____

The Clothes I Wear To School Are...

_____

_____

This Year, I Will Try To Get Better At...

_____

_____

The Things I Learned This Year Are...

_____

_____

_____

Other Activities I Would Like To Part Of Are...

_____

_____

_____

Next Year, I Am Looking Forward To...

_____

_____

_____

Draw Your Awesome Memory This School Year

Attach Pictures Of Fun Moments

KINDERGARTEN

School Year

_____

School

_____

Attach Your Photo

This School Year, I Am Looking Forward To...

_____

_____

My Teacher's Name is

_____

The Things I Bring To School Are...

_____

_____

_____

When I Arrive At School, The First Thing I Do Is...

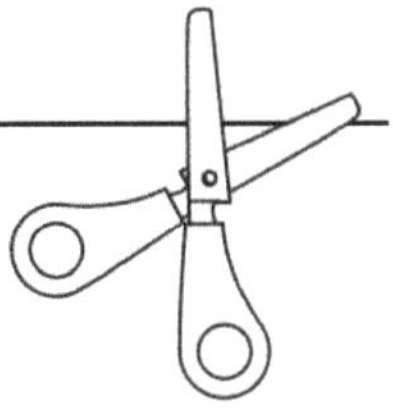

_____

_____

During Recess, I...

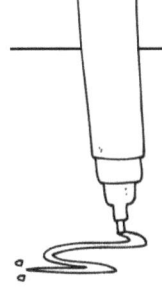

My Favorite Games To Play Are

_____

_____

My New Friends This Year Are...

_____

_____

The Clothes I Wear To School Are...

_____

_____

This Year, I Will Try To Get Better At...

_____

_____

The Things I Learned This Year Are...

_____

_____

_____

Other Activities I Would Like To Part Of Are...

_____

_____

_____

Next Year, I Am Looking Forward To...

_____

_____

_____

Draw Your Awesome Memory This School Year

Attach Pictures Of Fun Moments

GRADE 1
School Year

_____

School

_____

Attach Your Photo

This School Year, I Am Looking Forward To...

_____

_____

_____

My Teacher's Name is

_____

The Things I Bring To School Are...

_____

_____

_____

When I Arrive At School, The First Thing I Do Is...

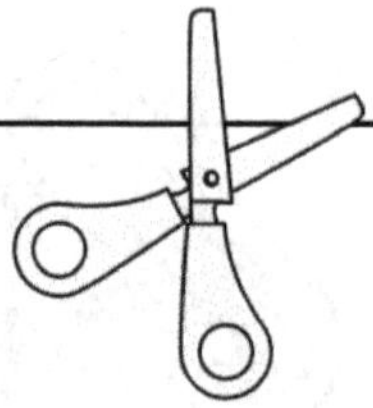

_____

_____

During Recess, I...

_____

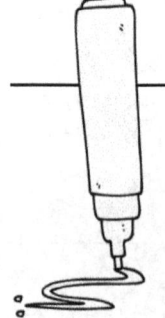

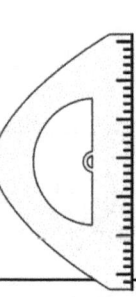

My Favorite Games To Play Are

_____

_____

My New Friends This Year Are...

_____

_____

The Clothes I Wear To School Are...

_____

_____

This Year, I Will Try To Get Better At...

_____

_____

The Things I Learned This Year Are...

_____

_____

_____

Other Activities I Would Like To Part Of Are...

_____

_____

_____

Next Year, I Am Looking Forward To...

_____

_____

_____

Draw Your Awesome Memory This School Year

Attach Pictures Of Fun Moments

GRADE 2

School Year

_____

School

_____

Attach Your Photo

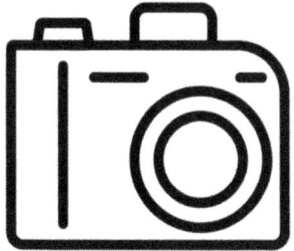

This School Year, I Am Looking Forward To...

_____

_____

My Teacher's Name is

_____

The Things I Bring To School Are...

_____

_____

_____

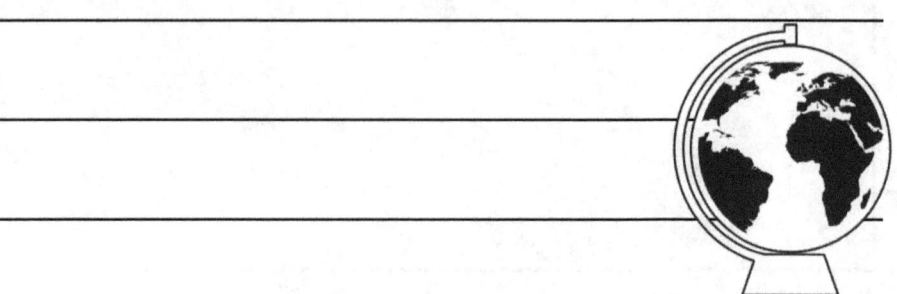

When I Arrive At School, The First Thing I Do Is...

_____

_____

During Recess, I...

_____

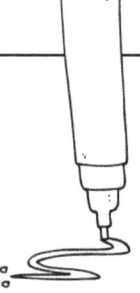

My Favorite Games To Play Are

_____

_____

My New Friends This Year Are...

_____

_____

The Clothes I Wear To School Are...

_____

_____

This Year, I Will Try To Get Better At...

_____

_____

The Things I Learned This Year Are...

_____

_____

_____

Other Activities I Would Like To Part Of Are...

_____

_____

_____

Next Year, I Am Looking Forward To...

_____

_____

_____

Draw Your Awesome Memory This School Year

Attach Pictures Of Fun Moments

GRADE 3
School Year

_____

School

_____

Attach Your Photo

This School Year, I Am Looking Forward To...

_____

_____

My Teacher's Name is

_____

The Things I Bring To School Are...

_____

_____

When I Arrive At School, The First Thing I Do Is...

_____

_____

_____

During Recess, I...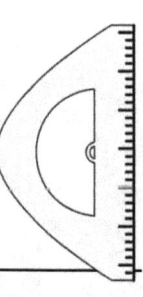

_____

_____

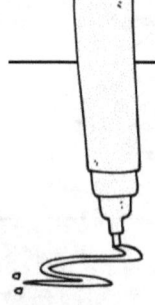

My Favorite Games To Play Are

_____

_____

My New Friends This Year Are...

_____

_____

_____

The Clothes I Wear To School Are...

_____

_____

_____

This Year, I Will Try To Get Better At...

_____

_____

_____

The Things I Learned This Year Are...

_____

_____

_____

Other Activities I Would Like To Part Of Are...

_____

_____

_____

Next Year, I Am Looking Forward To...

_____

_____

_____

Draw Your Awesome Memory This School Year

Attach Pictures Of Fun Moments

GRADE 4

School Year

_____

School

_____

Attach Your Photo

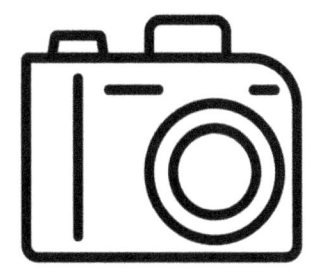

This School Year, I Am Looking Forward To...

_____

_____

My Teacher's Name is.

_____

The Things I Bring To School Are...

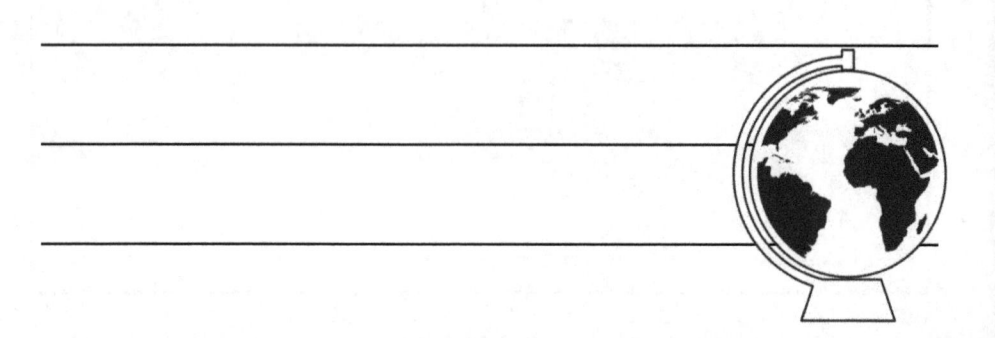

_____

_____

_____

When I Arrive At School, The First Thing I Do Is...

_____

_____

During Recess, I...

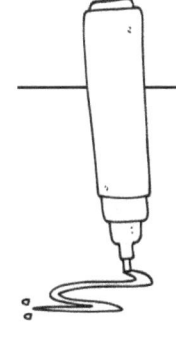

_____

_____

My Favorite Games To Play Are

_____

_____

My New Friends This Year Are...

_____

_____

The Clothes I Wear To School Are...

_____

_____

This Year, I Will Try To Get Better At...

_____

_____

The Things I Learned This Year Are...

_____

_____

Other Activities I Would Like To Part Of Are...

_____

_____

Next Year, I Am Looking Forward To...

_____

_____

Draw Your Awesome Memory This School Year

Attach Pictures Of Fun Moments

GRADE 5

School Year

_____

School

_____

Attach Your Photo

This School Year, I Am Looking Forward To...

_____

_____

_____

My Teacher's Name is

_____

The Things I Bring To School Are...

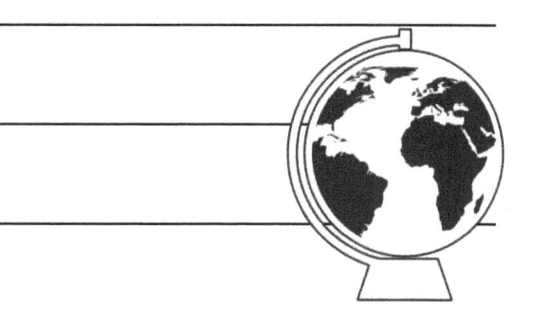

_____

_____

_____

When I Arrive At School, The First Thing I Do Is...

_____

_____

During Recess, I...

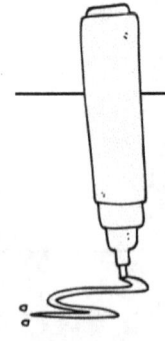

_____

_____

My Favorite Games To Play Are

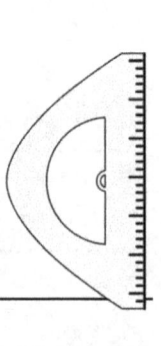

_____

_____

Draw Your Awesome Memory This School Year

Attach Pictures Of Fun Moments

GRADE 6

School Year

School

Attach Your Photo

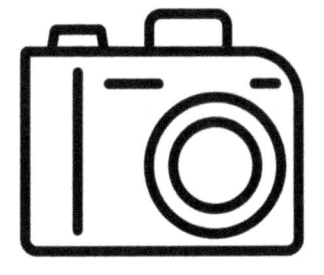

This School Year, I Am Looking Forward To...

_____

_____

My Teacher's Name is

_____

The Things I Bring To School Are...

_____

_____

_____

When I Arrive At School, The First Thing I Do Is...

_____

_____

During Recess, I...

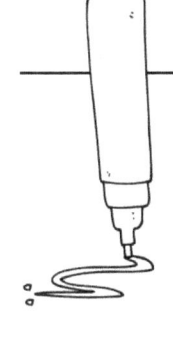

_____

_____

My Favorite Games To Play Are

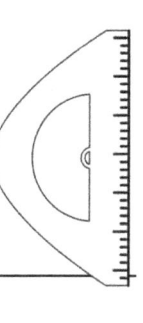

_____

_____

My New Friends This Year Are...

_____

_____

The Clothes I Wear To School Are...

_____

_____

This Year, I Will Try To Get Better At...

_____

_____

The Things I Learned This Year Are...

_____

_____

_____

Other Activities I Would Like To Part Of Are...

_____

_____

_____

Next Year, I Am Looking Forward To...

_____

_____

_____

Draw Your Awesome Memory This School Year

Attach Pictures Of Fun Moments

GRADE 7
School Year

_____

School

_____

Attach Your Photo

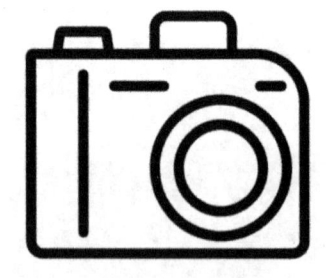

This School Year, I Am Looking Forward To...

_____

_____

_____

My Teacher's Name is

_____

The Things I Bring To School Are...

_____

_____

_____

When I Arrive At School, The First Thing I Do Is...

_____

_____

_____

During Recess, I...

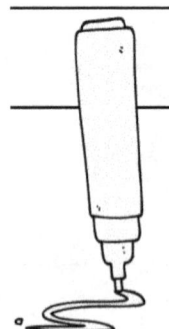

_____

_____

My Favorite Games To Play Are

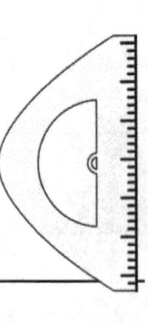

_____

_____

_____

My New Friends This Year Are...

_____

_____

The Clothes I Wear To School Are...

_____

_____

This Year, I Will Try To Get Better At...

_____

_____

The Things I Learned This Year Are...

_____

_____

_____

Other Activities I Would Like To Part Of Are...

_____

_____

_____

Next Year, I Am Looking Forward To...

_____

_____

_____

Draw Your Awesome Memory This School Year

Attach Pictures Of Fun Moments

GRADE 8

School Year

_____

School

_____

Attach Your Photo

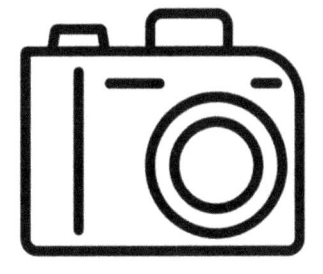

This School Year, I Am Looking Forward To...

_____

_____

My Teacher's Name is

_____

The Things I Bring To School Are...

_____

_____

_____

When I Arrive At School, The First Thing I Do Is...

_____

_____

During Recess, I...

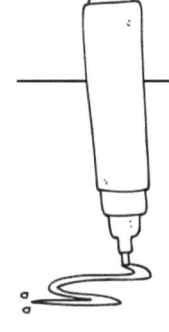

_____

_____

My Favorite Games To Play Are

_____

_____

My New Friends This Year Are...

_____

_____

The Clothes I Wear To School Are...

_____

_____

This Year, I Will Try To Get Better At...

_____

_____

The Things I Learned This Year Are...

_____

_____

_____

Other Activities I Would Like To Part Of Are...

_____

_____

_____

Next Year, I Am Looking Forward To...

_____

_____

_____

Draw Your Awesome Memory This School Year

Attach Pictures Of Fun Moments

GRADE 9
School Year

_____

School

_____

Attach Your Photo

This School Year, I Am Looking Forward To...

_____

_____

_____

My Teacher's Name is

_____

The Things I Bring To School Are...

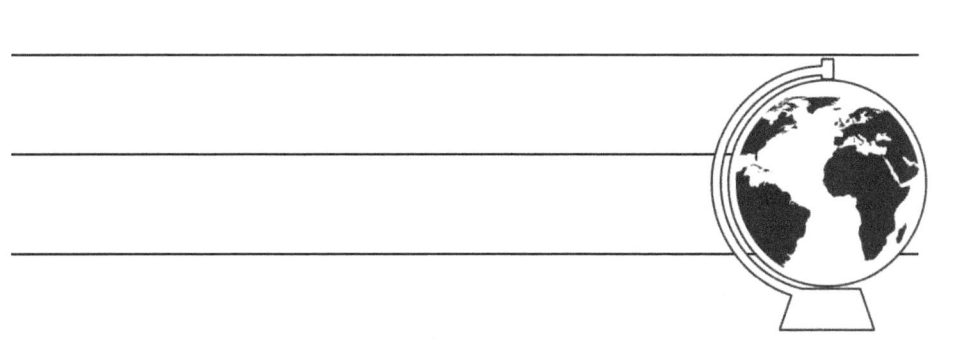

_____

_____

_____

_____

When I Arrive At School, The First Thing I Do Is...

_____

_____

During Recess, I...

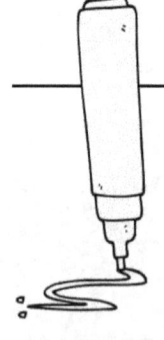

_____

_____

My Favorite Games To Play Are

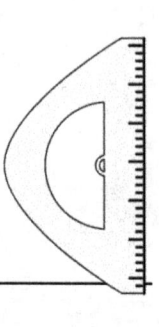

_____

_____

My New Friends This Year Are...

_____

_____

The Clothes I Wear To School Are...

_____

_____

This Year, I Will Try To Get Better At...

_____

_____

The Things I Learned This Year Are...

_____

_____

Other Activities I Would Like To Part Of Are...

_____

_____

Next Year, I Am Looking Forward To...

_____

_____

Draw Your Awesome Memory This School Year

Attach Pictures Of Fun Moments

GRADE 10

School Year

_____

School

_____

Attach Your Photo

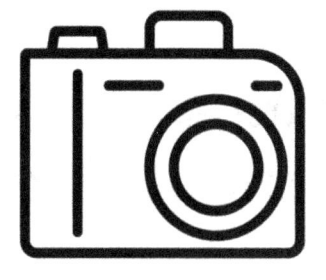

This School Year, I Am Looking Forward To...

_____

_____

My Teacher's Name is

_____

The Things I Bring To School Are...

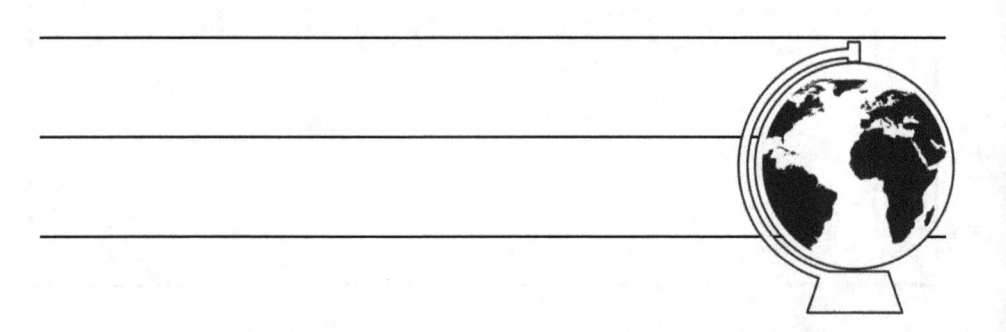

_____

_____

GRADE 10

School Year

_____

School

_____

Attach Your Photo

This School Year, I Am Looking Forward To...

_____

_____

My Teacher's Name is

_____

The Things I Bring To School Are...

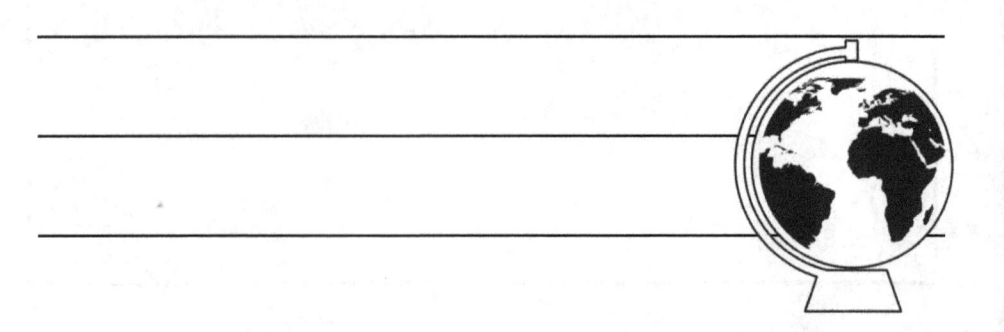

_____

_____

When I Arrive At School, The First Thing I Do Is...

_____

_____

_____

During Recess, I...

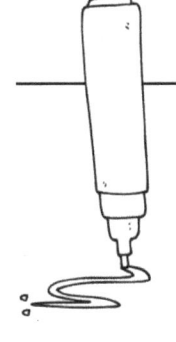

_____

_____

My Favorite Games To Play Are

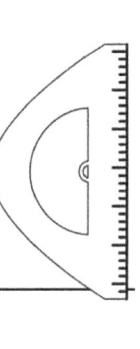

_____

_____

My New Friends This Year Are...

_____

_____

The Clothes I Wear To School Are...

_____

_____

This Year, I Will Try To Get Better At...

_____

_____

The Things I Learned This Year Are...

_____

_____

Other Activities I Would Like To Part Of Are...

_____

_____

Next Year, I Am Looking Forward To...

_____

_____

Draw Your Awesome Memory This School Year

Attach Pictures Of Fun Moments

GRADE 11

School Year

_____

School

_____

Attach Your Photo

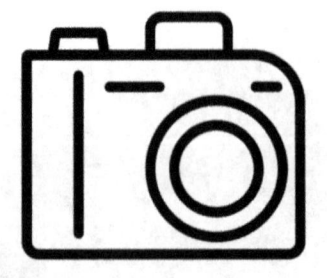

Attach Pictures Of Fun Moments

GRADE 11

School Year

_____

School
_____

Attach Your Photo

This School Year, I Am Looking Forward To...

_____

_____

My Teacher's Name is

_____

The Things I Bring To School Are...

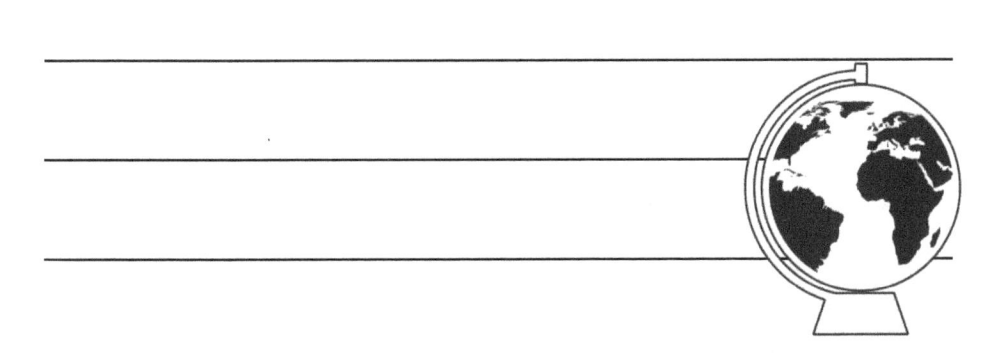

_____

_____

_____

When I Arrive At School, The First Thing I Do Is...

_____

_____

_____

During Recess, I...

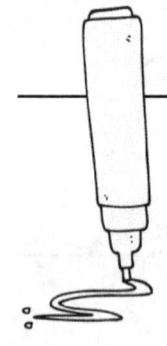

_____

_____

My Favorite Games To Play Are

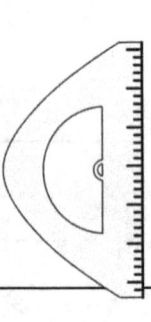

_____

_____

My New Friends This Year Are...

_____

_____

The Clothes I Wear To School Are...

_____

_____

This Year, I Will Try To Get Better At...

_____

_____

The Things I Learned This Year Are...

_____

_____

_____

Other Activities I Would Like To Part Of Are...

_____

_____

_____

Next Year, I Am Looking Forward To...

_____

_____

_____

Draw Your Awesome Memory This School Year

Attach Pictures Of Fun Moments

GRADE 12

School Year

_____

School

_____

Attach Your Photo

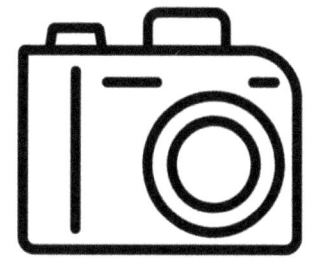

This School Year, I Am Looking Forward To...

_____

_____

_____

My Teacher's Name is

_____

The Things I Bring To School Are...

_____

_____

_____

_____

When I Arrive At School, The First Thing I Do Is...

_____

_____

During Recess, I...

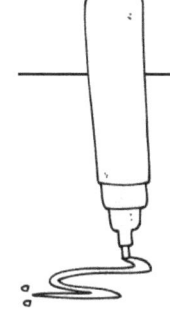

_____

_____

My Favorite Games To Play Are

_____

_____

My New Friends This Year Are...

_____

_____

The Clothes I Wear To School Are...

_____

_____

This Year, I Will Try To Get Better At...

_____

_____

The Things I Learned This Year Are...

_____

_____

_____

Other Activities I Would Like To Part Of Are...

_____

_____

_____

Next Year, I Am Looking Forward To...

_____

_____

_____

Draw Your Awesome Memory This School Year

Attach Pictures Of Fun Moments

Sign up for
Exclusive Offers
at
rebrand.ly/HJP

hobbyjournalpublishing.com

CPSIA information can be obtained
at www.ICGtesting.com
Printed in the USA
LVHW020303140423
744369LV00011B/314

9 798676 963361